Island Life

By Joanne Sinclair

MW00333264

CELEBRATION PRESS
Pearson Learning Group

Contents

Los Roques Islands, Venezuela

What Is an Island?

An island is a piece of land completely surrounded by water. Islands are found all over the world. They can be large or small. Islands can be countries, such as Iceland and Jamaica. They can also be part of countries, such as the island state of Tasmania in Australia and the island state of Hawaii in the United States.

Islands have a wide variety of **climates**. Jamaica, for example, is warm and sunny with sandy beaches and palm trees. Greenland is very cold. The ground is covered with ice and snow for much of the year. New Zealand has warm and cold climates.

The city of Hobart is on the island state of Tasmania, which lies off the south coast of mainland Australia.

Environment and climate are two things that can make an island different from other places. An island can also have a unique ecosystem. An ecosystem is all the living things in a particular environment. An island may have plants and animals that are not found anywhere else because the island is separated from other land.

Lemurs are found in the wild only on the island of Madagascar.

The largest island is Greenland.
One of the smallest islands is Bishop Rock.
It only has room for a lighthouse.

Ilulissat, Greenland

Bishop Rock, United Kingdom

The people living on an island may have their own unique language, culture, and **currency**. On some large islands, there are cities and towns. These provide jobs for the people who live there. People on smaller islands may have to work and buy food on the mainland, the nearest large body of land. On some islands, many people work in **tourism** or **conservation**.

Have you ever visited an island? Perhaps you live on one. This book will take you on a tour of four islands: Jamaica, the Galápagos Islands, New Zealand, and Prince Edward Island.

Islands on the Tour

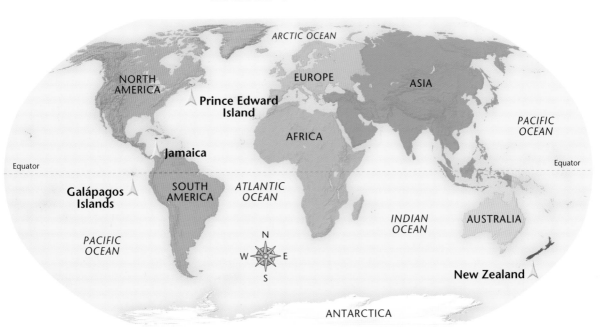

Jamaica

We begin our journey on the island country of Jamaica. Jamaica is in the Caribbean Sea, south of the United States and Cuba. It is the third largest island in the Caribbean Sea.

Tourists from all over the world visit Jamaica. It has a warm climate and beautiful landscapes. There are rain forests, rivers, waterfalls, and white beaches. Jamaica is also famous for its many mountains. In fact, Jamaica was formed from the tops of undersea mountain ranges.

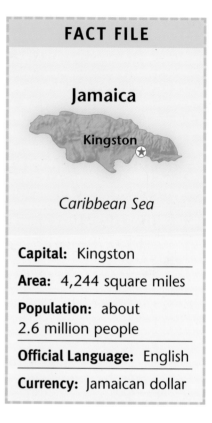

FACT FILE

Jamaica

Kingston

Caribbean Sea

Capital: Kingston

Area: 4,244 square miles

Population: about 2.6 million people

Official Language: English

Currency: Jamaican dollar

Jamaica's Blue Mountains

Jamaican guavas and pineapples are shipped to many countries.

Tropical plants grow well in Jamaica because of the hot, wet weather. Pineapples and guavas are two tropical fruits that grow there. Jamaica also has 3,000 varieties of flowers.

There are at least 200 different kinds of birds on the island. These include parakeets and pelicans. Bats, crocodiles, lizards, frogs, rats, and mongooses live in Jamaica, too.

The streamertail bird is only found in Jamaica.

Jamaica has been home to many different groups of people over the past few thousand years. Jamaican culture is now a mix of several different cultures. Today, most of the people are of **African descent**. The African influence can be heard in the music. Jamaican musicians have made steel drum bands, calypso, ska, and reggae music popular around the world.

Reggae Music
Reggae is a style of music that was first created in Jamaica in the late 1960s. An important feature of reggae is its strong, four-beat rhythm.
The rhythm is created by the drums, bass and electric guitars, and scraper, or ribbed stick.

The tops of oil drums are cut and tuned to use as steel drums by musicians on the island.

Jamaica's tropical climate allows people to grow several crops throughout the year. The islanders produce and sell sugar, bananas, coffee, and cocoa. Fishing and mining for bauxite (BAWK-syt), used to make aluminum, are important to Jamaica's economy. Tourism is also a source of jobs and income.

Coffee is grown in the Blue Mountains region in east Jamaica.

Fruits and vegetables grown on the island are sold in street markets.

Galápagos Islands

We now travel southwest to the Galápagos Islands. These islands were formed by underwater volcanoes along the **equator**. They are a province of Ecuador and are located about 600 miles off its coast in South America.

Places near the equator are usually hot and wet. The Galápagos Islands, however, have a drier and cooler climate. This is because the water around the islands is cool. It drifts up from icy Antarctica.

Thirteen main islands and six small islands make up the Galápagos.

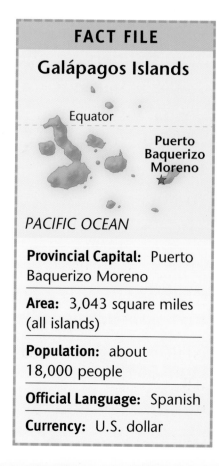

FACT FILE

Galápagos Islands

Equator — Puerto Baquerizo Moreno

PACIFIC OCEAN

Provincial Capital: Puerto Baquerizo Moreno

Area: 3,043 square miles (all islands)

Population: about 18,000 people

Official Language: Spanish

Currency: U.S. dollar

It is illegal to capture or remove giant tortoises or their eggs.

Some animals can only be found on the Galápagos Islands. The giant tortoise is one example. Some of these tortoises grow to five feet in length and can weigh hundreds of pounds. They can also live for more than 150 years.

Other unique animals include the fur seal and the marine iguana. The fur seal can grow to five feet long. People used to hunt the seal for its beautiful tan fur. This is now illegal. The marine iguana is the only sea lizard in the world. It spends its time on the Galápagos Islands' coastal rocks.

fur seal

The wildlife in the Galápagos Islands is special, so it needs to be protected. In 1959, Ecuador's government set aside the Galápagos Islands as a national park. Today, tourists from around the world come to see the unique wildlife. Tour groups are kept small to protect the unusual plants and animals. Visitors are also not allowed to touch the animals or get close to their resting places or nests.

Science of Survival
The scientist Charles Darwin (1809–1882) visited the Galápagos Islands in 1835. He saw how the wildlife on each island had special features. He wrote a book that explained how these plants and animals had changed, or evolved, over time to survive.

A tourist photographs two blue-footed boobies.

The capital, Puerto Baquerizo Moreno, is on the island of San Cristóbal.

People probably did not live on the Galápagos Islands until the 1500s. Few people live there today. This is because much of the land is protected. Huge hotels and cities are not allowed to be built there. People who do live on the islands often work with tourists or grow crops such as coffee and sugar. Scientists also live there studying the unique wildlife.

marine iguanas

New Zealand

Traveling southwest again, we come to the country of New Zealand. It lies south of the equator. It has two main islands: the North Island and the South Island. Millions of years ago, New Zealand may have been part of a larger **continent** that broke apart.

New Zealand is famous for its beautiful green landscape. It has rain forests, beaches, mountains, volcanoes, and **fiords** (fyordz). The North Island has volcanic hot springs and **geysers**.

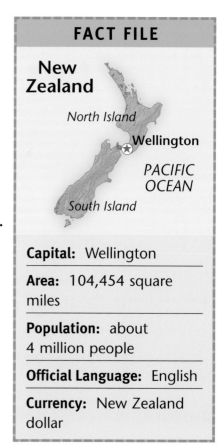

FACT FILE

New Zealand

North Island

Wellington

PACIFIC OCEAN

South Island

Capital: Wellington

Area: 104,454 square miles

Population: about 4 million people

Official Language: English

Currency: New Zealand dollar

Pohutu Geyser, North Island

The Southern Alps are on the South Island.

New Zealand's climate varies from north to south. The northern tip of the North Island is almost tropical. The most southern tip of the South Island is very cold.

Because of the variation in climate, New Zealand has many different kinds of plants and animals. The government has strict rules to protect them. The unique flightless bird, the kiwi, lives only in New Zealand.

The kiwi is one of New Zealand's national symbols.

The kiwi fruit is a small, oval fruit. It is eaten fresh or cooked.

New Zealand has different kinds of forests which include a variety of unique trees and plant life. The kauri (KOW-ree), a type of pine tree, is one of the largest trees in New Zealand. It's found in ancient forests. Some other plants found in New Zealand's forests include beech trees and giant tree ferns.

◄ Kauri trees can grow to more than 164 feet tall.

▲ The silver fern or ponga tree is a national symbol.

People have lived on New Zealand for about 1,200 years. The first people to settle the islands were the Maori (MOW-ree). Today, they make up one-fifth of the population. Many people have British **ancestors** because New Zealand was a British colony until 1947.

There are twenty times more farm animals than people in New Zealand. The grassy pastures are good for sheep and cattle grazing. Most of New Zealand's **exports** are farm products, such as meat, dairy products, and wool.

Most people in New Zealand live in towns and cities. Auckland, the largest city, is on the North Island.

Maori Welcome
The Maori have a special greeting called the Hongi. They press their foreheads and noses together to express friendship.

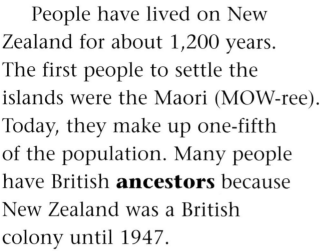

Prince Edward Island

We now travel halfway around the world to North America to get to Prince Edward Island. Prince Edward Island is a province of Canada. The island lies on Canada's east coast in the Gulf of St. Lawrence.

Viewed from the air, the island looks like a colorful patchwork quilt. The "quilt squares" are actually crops, such as potatoes and blueberries. The **fertile**, red soil makes the island ideal for farming.

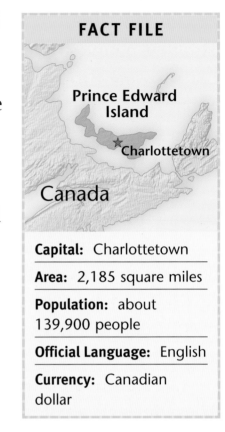

FACT FILE

Prince Edward Island

Charlottetown

Canada

Capital: Charlottetown

Area: 2,185 square miles

Population: about 139,900 people

Official Language: English

Currency: Canadian dollar

farmland, Prince Edward Island

18

Brackley Beach is a popular tourist resort on the island.

Prince Edward Island is not as warm as Jamaica, the Galápagos Islands, or the northern parts of New Zealand. It has cold winters and cool springs, and it is very popular with tourists. The island is known for its sand dunes and beaches.

The island is home to more than 300 species of birds. These include great blue herons, piping plovers, and bald eagles. Red squirrels, snowshoe hares, red foxes, minks, beavers, and muskrats can also be found on the island.

Piping plovers are endangered in North America.

Aboriginal people called the Mi'kmaq (MIHK-mak) came to the island more than 2,000 years ago. They were later joined by European settlers. The area then became a British colony. Today, Canada is an independent country. Prince Edward Island is one of its ten provinces.

Many of the people on the island work in farming. Other important industries are tourism, fishing, and **manufacturing**. The island also exports seafood.

Fishing boats line a harbor.

Lobsters are caught off the island's coast.

Canada's Birthplace

Charlottetown, the capital of Prince Edward Island, is known as Canada's birthplace. In 1864, it was the site of the first of several important meetings. The meetings led to Canada's independence from the United Kingdom in 1867.

Islands of the World

Islands exist in all parts of the world. They have different climates, ecosystems, and wildlife. People living on islands may have their own particular culture. This book has shown you just a few islands. Here are some more from around the world.

Greenland is the largest island in the world and is located in the northern Atlantic Ocean. Most of it is covered in ice. For a few weeks every summer, there is no night. In the winter, there is no daylight.

The **Maldives** are made up of about 1,200 tiny islands in the Indian Ocean. People live on about 200 of the islands. The islands are surrounded by coral reefs and have a tropical climate.

Madagascar lies off the southeast coast of Africa in the Indian Ocean. It is the world's fourth largest island. Its rain forests are home to unusual animals such as lemurs, chameleons, and geckoes.

Great Britain is made up of England, Scotland, and Wales. Together with Northern Ireland, a province on the neighboring island of Ireland, they form the United Kingdom. The capital is London, a densely populated city.

Japan is made up of four large, mountainous islands and over 1,000 smaller islands. It is located in the Pacific Ocean off the coast of eastern Asia. The capital, Tokyo, is one of the largest cities in the world.

Glossary

African descent having ancestors originally from Africa

ancestor someone who comes much earlier in a family, especially someone earlier than a grandparent

climates reoccurring weather conditions in particular places

conservation preservation of land, animals, and plants

continent one of the seven major land masses in the world: Africa, Antarctica, Asia, Australia, Europe, North America, and South America

currency the money that is commonly used in a country

equator an imaginary line around the middle of Earth, dividing the Northern and Southern Hemispheres

export goods sent to other countries for sale

fertile able to produce many fruits or crops

fiords deep, narrow waterways between steep cliffs, formed by the actions of glaciers

geyser an underground spring that shoots hot water and steam into the air from time to time

manufacturing making lots of goods or products, usually by using machines

tourism the business of providing services to people who are traveling for pleasure

tropical located in the warm region near the equator

Index

Panalu'u Beach Park, Big Island, Hawaii